ENTREPRENEURIAL SCOTLAND

PORTRAITS OF INSPIRATION

Photographs by Tricia Malley & Ross Gillespie
Words by Kenny Kemp

www.entrepreneurial-exchange.co.uk

First published in hardback in Great Britain in 2006 by The Entrepreneurial Exchange
Barncluith Business Centre, Townhead Street, Hamilton ML3 7DP

Project Manager – Angela Paterson

Creative and Production – Frame Creative

Typeset in Trajan and Stone Serif

Written by Kenny Kemp

Photography by Tricia Malley and Ross Gillespie, broad daylight ltd

Printed and bound in Scotland by Pillans & Waddies

A CIP catalogue record for this book is available from the British Library.

ISBN 0-9553199-7-8

ISBN 978-0-9553199-7-6

The contents of this book are an interpretation of the subjects, their personalities and their good will.
The book is not intended as a reference source for market and financial information.

CONTENTS

Foreword by Sir Richard Branson 5

Portraits of Inspiration: An Introduction by John Anderson 7

Entrepreneurial Scotland: An Overview by Kenny Kemp 9

Portraits of Inspiration 13

    Lord Macfarlane of Bearsden 14

    Sir Tom Hunter 16

    Sir Tom Farmer CBE 18

    Sir Jackie Stewart OBE 20

    John Boyle 22

    Brian Souter 24

    Richard Emanuel MBE 26

    Jim McColl OBE 28

    David Sibbald 30

    Sir Arnold Clark 32

    Willie Haughey OBE 34

    Ann Gloag OBE 36

    Sam Russell MBE 38

    Sir Ian Wood CBE 40

    Donald Macdonald OBE 42

    Moir Lockhead OBE 44

    Chris Gorman OBE 46

    Alasdair Locke 48

    Walter Nimmo 50

    Keith Miller CBE 52

    Gordon Baxter 54

    Sir Bill Gammell 56

Words of Inspiration 59

List of Members of The Entrepreneurial Exchange 61

ACKNOWLEDGEMENTS

The photographic portraits in this book by award-winning photographers Tricia Malley and Ross Gillespie attempt to capture the essence of each entrepreneur. There was no prescriptive, pre-conceived agenda, the aim was simply to show everyone as a unique human being, connecting their professional lives, where possible, with the images. We would like to thank the individuals for their co-operation and good humour which has helped fulfil this most exciting project.

The Exchange is also grateful for the contribution of journalist and author Kenny Kemp, twice Scotland's Business Writer of the Year, for his incisiveness and wit in creating such vivid verbal portraits of the crowded business lives depicted here. Our thanks go, too, to the Frame Creative team, in particular David Frame for the book's design and visual impact and Jim Middleton for his editing and layout skills.

Finally, credit must go to Angela Paterson who, as Project Manager, has been the driving force throughout; and to our Chief Executive John Anderson for his pivotal role in realising the Exchange's vision to produce this unique book.

FOREWORD

I'VE ALWAYS HAD AN ADMIRATION FOR THE SCOTS. After all, I married a beautiful one from Glasgow – and I've had more than a few working with me at Virgin over the years. I appreciate that as individuals they have immense qualities and a ferocious work ethic. And most of them also enjoy having a bit of fun along the way.

I'm delighted to be asked to write the foreword to *Portraits of Inspiration*, because I know personally many of the people in this book and I find them inspiring Scottish entrepreneurs. And while the people featured in the following pages come from a variety of backgrounds they all share the common traits that I admire: business zeal, hard work, determination and inexhaustible energy.

I have watched the Scottish entrepreneur at work for many years. And as I travel the globe they pop up all the time in the most unexpected places. They are usually individuals who understand that the world is out there to be challenged and tamed. It is their spirit to succeed that seems to matter most.

But while the Scottish entrepreneur can be found in many habitats all over the world – I think it is even more special that many still choose to live and work in their own homeland. And I also include here the entrepreneurs who have settled in Scotland as their adopted home.

Scotland is a small, almost perfectly-formed nation, so entrepreneurs have to move beyond the geographical barriers of birth to make their fortunes. I understand why every one of the entrepreneurs featured in this book has made their name – and picked up great business ideas along the way – from working outside of Scotland.

But there is also another important aspect I admire – the great tradition of Scottish philanthropy. While Andrew Carnegie is renowned as one of the world's great givers, I am proud that the present generation also views this as a priority too. Their passion to help those less fortunate all over the world is often greater than their business zeal.

I think this is an excellent and timely publication. I am proud to be a member of The Entrepreneurial Exchange Hall of Fame and I have made many friends among this illustrious group over the past 10 years. I'm sure it will act as a catalyst to inspire others. And I look forward to meeting many, many more Scottish entrepreneurs – and perhaps doing some business with them – over the coming years.

Sir Richard Branson

London, May 2006

PORTRAITS OF INSPIRATION: AN INTRODUCTION

WELCOME TO THIS CELEBRATION of Scotland's leading entrepreneurs. It is long overdue. Every one of the individuals featured in this book deserves their place in the Entrepreneurial Exchange Hall of Fame, nominated by their peers. Some are well-known faces whilst others have quietly built up their businesses away from the glare of publicity. Most were born in Scotland – others have chosen Scotland as their homeland. All make a significant contribution to this nation.

What is clear is that there isn't a magic formula for becoming a successful wealth creator. There are some obvious characteristics, with raw determination and a quest for learning being common themes, but every one of our subjects is unique and I believe they are all worthy ambassadors for enterprising Scotland.

The Entrepreneurial Exchange's initial idea for this collection was to show that in modern Scotland there is now a significant band of inspirational role models for our young people. That hasn't always been the case.

Back in 1989, I returned to Scotland from Chicago to find our country an apparent entrepreneurial wilderness. I was determined to seek out people who were actively driving their businesses forward in Scotland. There was no obvious meeting place, no listing or directory and little media interest but over the next few years I began to find them and in the summer of 1994 wrote my MBA thesis *Local Heroes – Scotland's Entrepreneurial Role Models*. One key finding – that entrepreneurs wanted advice from other entrepreneurs – was published in Alastair Balfour's new magazine in November 1994. Also in that magazine was an article describing a new organisation to be created in Lanarkshire *"for entrepreneurs, by entrepreneurs"* – this was The Entrepreneurial Exchange.

So the wealth creators were there and now they had an organisation to encourage and support them.

Since its inception nearly 12 years ago much has been achieved. Indeed, the entrepreneur is enjoying something of a revival. Our television channels have discovered what we have known all along: most wealth creators are imaginative, decisive and driven. Indeed, they have compelling personalities that make interesting viewing. *Portraits of Inspiration* is intended to give a flavour of their diversity and seeks to identify some of the reasons for success. I hope you enjoy both the portraits and words.

The Entrepreneurial Exchange is immensely proud of its contribution to a modern Scotland. We remain focused on providing ambitious entrepreneurs in Scotland with the opportunity to meet and learn from like-minded people. What is exciting is that a new generation is now on the way. I look ahead with anticipation to Volume Two!

John Anderson

Chief Executive of The Entrepreneurial Exchange

ENTREPRENEURIAL SCOTLAND: AN OVERVIEW

A THREAD OF SILVER AND GOLD runs through the rich tapestry of Scotland's economic history. For the derring-do of the mercantile classes has embroidered much of the nation's familiar landscape with their legacies.

From the Mediaeval traders shipping coal to the Low Countries to Jinglin' Geordie, the Royal jeweller and goldsmith who followed James VI and First down to London in 1603; from the Tobacco Lords, such as Glassford, to the Iron, Coal and Shipbuilding barons and to Andrew Carnegie and beyond, the men of money have made their mark on the world.

And Scotland's growing cities prospered – especially Glasgow, Edinburgh and Dundee. TC Smout in *A History of the Scottish People* says: "The greatness of Glasgow was built upon the entrepreneurial skill of her businessmen, whether merchants or manufacturers. Enterprise and resilience had been their noted attributes over a long period."

It was not just the swashbuckling merchants with their eyes on the West Indies and America but domestic manufacturers establishing sugar refineries, cloth factories, soapworks, distilleries, all in a ferocious spirit of industry.

Smout says: "The pioneer industrialist not only carried the burden of developing the economy of Glasgow. They were also laying the foundations of a new Scottish economic order, and in so doing, affected the lives of all who have lived since."

But after the prolonged boom of the railways and the Victorian age, Scotland seemed to turn its back on its industrial heroes, spiralling into a nation where wealth creation became the antithesis of national achievement and increasingly a cause for resentment and class envy.

Perhaps the rapacious behaviour of some isolated business figures didn't help, but it was a sad reflection on the Scots, after all the greatest industrialists often emerged from humble beginnings, inspired by empirical learning and the chance of fame and fortune furth of the Tweed.

There was a good reason why the Scots were renowned for their adaptability and ingenuity – the universal education system instilled a sense of pride and purpose.

George Miller, the first biographer of Scotland, tells the traveller not to be surprised when he comes to Scotland. "However humble their condition, the peasantry can all read and are generally more or less skilful in writing and arithmetic, and under the disguise of their uncouth appearance … they possess a laudable zeal for knowledge … not generally found among the same class of men in other countries in Europe."

This helped Scotland become not only a nation of scientists, engineers, inventors, teachers, administrators, architects and philosophers but also of business people. The Scottish people became the country's greatest single asset.

But since the Second World War, only a determined pocket of successful business figures have carried a beacon for enterprise while large tracts of the nation appeared mired in self-pity and an acute lack of ambition.

There was a need to prove that Scotland was more than a land of hills and glens, tartan, haggis and whisky. There was a requirement to demonstrate that Scotland was still capable of producing great national and international people of business and commerce.

By the early 1990s there was an increasing awareness of the value and significance of the entrepreneur to Scotland, and a more positive shift towards their wider acceptance by Scots. Even the word itself, derived from the French for anyone with the drive to run something, was becoming more widely recognised, although it doesn't exactly trip off the Scottish tongue.

But while Scotland's financial sector was able to boast of its world-leading credentials, there were precious few modern Scots entrepreneurs operating on the world stage. This needed to be tackled, yet there would be no overnight fix. And there was a need for a broader definition.

So what do we mean by an entrepreneur and what does such a person actually do? Was there a formula for success? And how could new entrepreneurs be encouraged to aspire to greater heights? What, indeed, was holding us back? This became the rationale for the creation of a unique Scottish organisation – now admired around the world.

The idea for The Entrepreneurial Exchange as an organisation *"for entrepreneurs, by entrepreneurs"* was developed in 1994 by economic development body Lanarkshire Development Agency. With the active support of Terry Currie, project manager Ewen Macaulay worked on initial plans with a steering group of entrepreneurs, chaired initially by Bill Fleming. The nature of The Entrepreneurial Exchange as a not-for-profit membership organisation was established with an original aim of fostering the culture of entrepreneurship in Scotland. A key was going to be the recruitment of founder members – successful role models who would agree to share their experiences of growing a business with those who had yet to make it. The opening gambit was achieved in January 1995 when 20 entrepreneurs attended the first meeting of founder members.

Sir Tom Hunter now recalls: "I had just bought the sports business Olympus at this time and the guys came to me and asked me to join them. I thought I had more to learn than to give at the time.

"From day one, I felt excited because the founders were trying to do something I was genuinely interested in," Hunter remembers. "It was an opportunity to meet like-minded people and, on that score, it hasn't really changed."

From the start The Entrepreneurial Exchange captured the imagination of Scotland's wealth creators. It brought together multi-millionaires with decades of success under their belts with the raw, wide-eyed hopefuls steering towards their first deals. But there was a chemistry that seemed to work.

Under the chairmanship of, firstly, Professor Ron Lander, then Donald Storrie and later Rita Rusk, The Entrepreneurial Exchange developed its unique programme of events and support for the ambitious entrepreneur in Scotland. The team of Jacqueline Walker, Kirsty Campbell and Karen Stewart in the Exchange office ensured that the increasing number of members were catered for, organising events and making introductions. Sub-committees of the board enthusiastically took on the jobs of running annual awards dinners and spring conferences.

In 2000, Tom Hunter was elected as chairman and the board was invited to an away-day brainstorming session in Cameron House Hotel on the shores of Loch Lomond to come up with a strategy for the burgeoning Exchange, now with several hundred members across Scotland. If the Exchange had a future as a credible force, it needed a sharper set of goals.

"The most significant thing that happened during my chairmanship was bringing in John Anderson as Chief Executive. Before his arrival it had been run with a lot of goodwill and pulling in favours from members but with no real dedication of resource. It was a typical entrepreneurial thing. Just get it started and we'll sort out the detail later."

Anderson was the ideal appointment. Having lived in Chicago, he had first hand experience of how a culture of entrepreneurship and risk taking could impact on an economy. He had been involved with the Exchange since 1995, initially behind the scenes and then as a board member, and was an acknowledged expert in Scotland's entrepreneurial culture as a result of his *Local Heroes* work.

"We sat down and worked out what we actually did as an organisation and how we could be more effective. We took a good look at our membership to see how they could help," says Hunter.

The Exchange redefined what it was doing – and who it wanted to help, remembering that the original tagline was: *"for entrepreneurs, by entrepreneurs."* This wasn't a cosy PR slogan, this was about rolling up the sleeves and taking part. A refreshed mission statement was developed: "The Entrepreneurial Exchange will lead the drive to make Scotland a more entrepreneurial and confident society for the benefit of all." The key objectives were to inform, motivate, educate, inspire and support entrepreneurs.

The process defined three broad communities of members: those who were at an early stage in business with up to £1 million turnover, those at the next level with £1 million to £5 million turnover, and those with £5 million and above. The Exchange put together programmes of events to suit the various stages of growth of a business. Entrepreneurs would give their time to run workshops, talk at dinners and suppers, where unique issues would be thrashed out in private – usually with a decent meal at the end of it.

"It was interesting how the Exchange broke naturally into thirds and we were more able to tailor our help and advice to these communities," says John Anderson.

One of the stated aims was to help those who really wanted to grow their businesses. "Somebody who has two shops, and happy to stay with that, isn't really the kind of member we are looking for – they will not face the same growing pains as the ambitious entrepreneur."

Exchange Honorary President Sir Tom Farmer believes that The Entrepreneurial Exchange has played a strong role in changing attitudes to wealth creators in Scotland.

"The great thing about Scotland was this sense of community. Entrepreneurs were willing to give up their time to help others. They were being asked to take time out of their busy business schedules to give advice and speak at events," he says.

Brian Souter is a figure who recognises that the Exchange has helped give entrepreneurs a common voice. "It is tremendously important to Scotland now. It has done a lot to change the public's perception. There is a new generation coming through and they can take on the mantle from the older guard, like me."

Very rarely have members turned down requests to share experience and give a commitment. This has nurtured a sense of community and a genuine feeling of responsibility to the forthcoming generation of Scottish entrepreneurs.

"This is what makes the Exchange different; a lot of people are willing to give up their time and take part," says Tom Hunter.

But if Scotland's universal education system was the reason for past entrepreneurial glory, for the sake of Scotland's future, the Exchange felt it important to rekindle this fire by working with today's young people.

From the outset, the Exchange has worked closely with the Prince's Scottish Youth Business Trust, to encourage youthful entrepreneurs to raise their game, and with Young Enterprise Scotland in supporting their work in schools across the country. A broader commitment to help change the attitude and aspirations of the young people of Scotland saw the Exchange and its members provide significant support to the groundbreaking Schools Enterprise Programme in primary schools and to the recent expansion of these activities into secondary education through the Determined to Succeed strategy. Indeed the Exchange itself led with the creation of the School Link programme aimed at encouraging its members to partner with local schools. It has been an eye-opening and rewarding experience for both parties.

While there was an early reticence on the part of the teaching profession when Scotland's entrepreneurial community approached with a scheme to encourage more enterprise, significant progress has been made, winning over the head teachers and teachers as much as the pupils. Scotland's educators are now seeing clear proof that cutting into the busy curriculum to promote entrepreneurial activities is a worthwhile use of the school timetable.

The young Scot who chooses to continue their education beyond school will now find an established resource of entrepreneurial teaching and support throughout the higher education establishments of Scotland. Following the pioneering creation of the Centres for Entrepreneurship at Glasgow Caledonian University; Napier, Stirling and Robert Gordon Universities and the Universities of Aberdeen and Strathclyde, all higher education institutions in Scotland now have some form of entrepreneurship education, thanks to the pioneering work of the Scottish Institute for Enterprise. All over Scotland, Exchange members are helping to deliver inspirational learning experiences which will encourage Scotland's young people to consider new career options.

Today's breed of Scottish entrepreneur understands that their wealth carries with it certain responsibilities to society. This is the "give something back" element of the Exchange's informal credo: *"Work Hard, Play Hard, Give Something Back."*

These philanthropic tendencies are actively encouraged by the Exchange and members have shown their immense generosity again and again. Charities in Scotland and around the world have all benefited from the Exchange's contribution. It isn't complicated; after all, you can only ever own a certain number of cars and castles. Each member makes significant personal contributions to chosen charitable causes, but they are also inundated with requests for cash and help. They simply can't help them all; but most dig deep to help those less fortunate. A recent summer ball raised £1.8 million for Africa – a typical example of the Exchange's largesse and a tip in the iceberg of support.

So The Entrepreneurial Exchange is carrying a torch for a modern entrepreneurial and confident Scotland. Today, under the chairmanship of Jim McColl, that flame is burning bright and it will be rewarded if it manages to set alight more Scots with the ambition and zeal to succeed in their chosen fields.

Kenny Kemp

May 2006

PORTRAITS OF INSPIRATION

LORD MACFARLANE OF BEARSDEN

Hall of Fame | 1995

ONCE UPON A TIME A FIRM HANDSHAKE between two gentlemen was enough to start up a company in Scotland. No need for business plans, money-laundering checks and five-year projections. Just a look straight into the eyes to assess someone's honesty and desire to succeed.

Norman Macfarlane was a Royal Artillery officer invalided out after breaking his neck while serving in Palestine. During his convalescence in hospital he decided to set up a business. It was the beginning of a passionate affair that turned him into one of the UK's most distinguished industrialists. He is a Post-war colossus of Scottish business, with a catalogue brimful of fine achievements, among them his tenure as chairman of Distillers Company and then Guinness during the take-over storms.

But a meeting at the National Commercial Bank of Scotland in Glasgow in 1949 changed his life. "I had £400 demob money which was not enough to set up a company. So I arranged to go and see Mr Stirling, a nice man who eventually became the financial director of House of Fraser," recalls Lord Macfarlane.

Mr Stirling obviously took a shine to the articulate young man bristling with ambition and he arranged to give him £5,000, a substantial sum. And so N.S. Macfarlane & Co. Ltd was created. "Nobody ever said business plan or anything like that," recalls Lord Macfarlane.

Several decades later Lord Macfarlane became Deputy Chairman of Clydesdale Bank in Glasgow. "I used to remind the people in the bank that looking across the table into somebody's eyes was once a banker's skill. They didn't get it right all the time, but if they got it right the majority of times, the bank would grow."

Norman Macfarlane was astute. He could see that the booming Scotch whisky industry was moving away from heavy wooden crates. Corrugated cardboard boxes were a better way of shipping the goods and HM's Customs & Excise insisted that every cardboard case of bottles must be sealed with self-adhesive tape.

"I realised there was going to be a big market for printed adhesive tape. A few people were playing with it but nobody in the country had the machinery. It was very difficult to print because the adhesive would remove the print. I went across to Philadelphia to buy two machines and installed them in Woodlands Terrace in Glasgow. At that time I was the only one in Scotland who could print self-adhesive, printed tape."

This was where Lord Macfarlane's knowledge of the whisky business took off. He looked at making bottle tops and packaging, his company finding ways of saving costs and improving a host of household products. Soon he was making money with a string of acquisitions to follow and he set up the Macfarlane Group (Clansman) in 1973, still a Scottish listed company. But his high-wire challenges came in steering United Distillers as chairman from 1987 until 1996, and as chairman of Guinness during the major City battles of 1987-1989. Guinness became global drinks company Diageo, makers of Johnnie Walker and Smirnoff, the world's leading Scotch whisky and vodka brands. Lord Macfarlane, elevated as a Conservative peer, remains Diageo's Honorary Life President.

Art remains another enduring passion – he has been a discerning private and corporate collector for 50 years, supporting many Scottish artists. He is also proud of his leadership of the Kelvingrove Museum and Art Gallery in Glasgow restoration fund – "a place I have loved since I was a boy when I went regularly with my father."

"I used to remind the people that looking across the table into somebody's eyes was once a banker's skill."

SIR TOM HUNTER

Hall of Fame | 1996

TOM HUNTER IS A GIFTED HUMAN BEING. An Ayrshire son, he has many outstanding qualities and is one of Scotland's most inspirational business figures, admired on a global stage. But his tungsten-steel strengths are as a loyal partner and collaborator, a communicator of new ideas, and as a conscientious entrepreneur.

He has a heightened sense of teaming up with the right people for the right projects. Timing is important too. And while that instinct might have deserted him now and then, he has seldom put a designer sports shoe in the wrong place. Certainly he has avoided the pitfalls of corporate life.

While many entrepreneurs are portrayed as maverick operators, cranky, sour and difficult to handle, Sir Tom is a banana and mango smoothie. That doesn't equate to being a push-over. Far from it, because he drives a ferocious bargain. And, while he wants to do well on a personal level, he also wants Scotland to succeed, and to embrace a true culture of enterprise.

"The biggest question we still debate is: being a successful entrepreneur, is it about nature or nurture. The answer I have come to is it is a bit of both. There are natural-born entrepreneurs, the Bransons and the Philip Greens, but I believe with the right education and nurturing, more people can give it a real go."

Tom Hunter's belief is that everyone can be a bit better. Education is the key that unlocks this door. Not just for the emerging generation, but also for Scotland's teachers and educators, who he feels have a vital part to play in instilling the ethos of success and achievement.

Hunter's success has been in the retail leisure and sports business. His shops sell items that make people feel good; from fashion sports shoes to jeans and T-shirts. So he doesn't want to be too po-faced about life. He's got a sense of humour and the ability to have a real laugh at himself. His motto captures the spirit of entrepreneurship in Scotland: work hard, play hard and give something back.

There's another strand to his wealth though: commercial property investment; and, more recently, he has been eyeing up even more opportunities. These have brought him close ties with billionaires Philip Green, the Barclay Brothers, and the Reuben Brothers. While he deals in such rarefied UK business circles, more recently he has turned his mind to venture philanthropy, where wealth is being channelled back into appropriate projects to encourage and inspire.

As one of Scotland's richest men he has consistently put his money back into dozens of worthy causes, such as the Hunter Foundation, working in Africa, and the Hunter Centre for Entrepreneurship at Strathclyde University. His generosity includes a £6 million contribution to the restored Kelvingrove Art Gallery and Museum, to set up a room in honour of his father, Campbell.

Like so many celebrated entrepreneurs, he remains driven and focused on achievement for himself and his homeland. Scotland needs to clone more Tom Hunters.

"I believe with the right education and nurturing, more people can give it a real go."

SIR TOM FARMER OBE

Hall of Fame | 1996

SIR TOM FARMER IS ARGUABLY SCOTLAND'S best known entrepreneur. Sir Tom made a virtue out of the personal touch – he still does.

His face and name were displayed on advertising billboards throughout the country and his smiling physiognomy proved assuring to millions of car owners. When Kwik-Fit, the tyre and exhaust business, was sold to Ford for £1 billion in 2000, Sir Tom left with considerable wealth. His success became part of Scottish folklore ... how the chirpy lad who left school at 15 to sweep the floors in a tyre delivery firm became an outstanding international business figure.

"When the word entrepreneur was first used to describe someone like myself, I wondered what it actually meant – was this a good or bad description? The more you asked people and the more dictionaries you consulted, the more different and varied meanings you got," says Sir Tom.

"I decided that I would set out my own definition. For me, an entrepreneur is somebody who sees an opportunity and is able to reach out and grasp it for their own benefit – the benefit of their family, their business – and very importantly, for the benefit of the community."

This is a comfortable description for the man from Leith who nearly retired aged 28 having sold his first car accessory business for an amount which would have given him and his family sound financial security. Tom and his wife Anne and their two children Sally and John headed out to sunny California in 1970; however, he eventually became frustrated with the lack of any business challenge and decided to return to Scotland, and ... the rest is the Kwik-Fit story.

Sir Tom says not everyone will have the desire to go out and start their own business – that just does not happen. However, what we want to do is to encourage and develop the "can-do" entrepreneurial attitude.

"It is not just in the business world where we want people with vision and high energy, but every sector of life is looking for entrepreneurs. We need the desired spirit in health service, in education, the civil service and other public services.

"If you are lucky enough to be born with good genes and high energy, then you've got a good start in life." This isn't the glucose Mars Bar diet though – this high-energy is inherent in Sir Tom – even today.

"I was fortunate to be born into a tremendously supportive family and community, with people from an early age in my life encouraging me, and always urging me to do my best. I had the security of knowing that everyone who surrounded me cared and encouraged me and this has continued throughout my life. "

Sir Tom has been a long-term philanthropist; helping in Africa, his Church, and many local and national communities.

He is proud of his Papal Knighthood and was touched by the spirituality of Mother Teresa and the Dalai Lama. Those people and other great leaders of the World preach the same basic principles: "Respect your God and ... respect your fellow-man."

"For me, an entrepreneur is somebody who sees an opportunity and is able to reach out and grasp it for their own benefit – the benefit of their family, their business – and very importantly, for the benefit of the community."

SIR JACKIE STEWART OBE

Hall of Fame | 1997

JACKIE STEWART THRIVES ON CONTROVERSIAL POINTS.

"You know winning is not enough ... Not a bad statement," he says before repeating it. "Winning is not enough. Lots of people can win. They can win for a short time or win a single event. Even the World Motor Racing Championship is not that difficult to win once," he says.

He then qualifies his statement. "What is more difficult – and it is in a different class altogether – is long-term success. To be successful is much more than being a winner. Because nobody wins all the time, but success is being able to come back and do it again ... and do it another time. And sustain it. To sustain success you've got to continue to deliver and you can't rest on your laurels."

Sir Jackie Stewart is a world-famous Scottish sporting icon. While the late Jimmy Johnstone was gracing the football field with his world beating team-mates, Jackie, wearing his famous Stewart tartan banded helmet, was delivering behind the steering wheel of a Tyrrell Formula One car.

Sir Jackie was anointed World Champion in 1969, repeating the feat in 1971 and again in 1973. He had guts, determination and a will to win in a profession where death was always chasing the pack.

"When the flag drops, the bullshit stops. You can pose and tell everyone how good you are, but when the flag drops you've got to deliver," he says referring to the national flag to start a Grand Prix, now a relic of the racing past.

"I mean, I won 27 Grands Prix but in fact I was only part of the team that won. And the reason was the car didn't break down. There's no point in winning pole position or the fastest lap; to finish first, first you must finish. I only won about 19 pole positions in my life but I won 27 Grands Prix because I spent most of the time setting the car up to win, not just to do it for one lap. So you need good people to do that."

When close friend and team-mate François Cévert perished in the US Grand Prix in 1973, the Scottish legend decided life was too precious and called it a day two weeks later.

He banked his winnings and moved effortlessly into a new career as an American television commentator, trading on his name. He kept hold of his lucrative contracts with his global, multinational, corporate sponsors. He made millions more in advertising as the Flying Scot. Despite his dyslexia, he set up a global business empire, working with the likes of the Ford Motor Company for more than 40 years, and then created a Formula One racing team. In Scotland, he turned his shooting prowess into a business success with his world famous centre at Gleneagles.

"I'm a man for detail. I like to consider every eventuality and assess every risk. In my view, this is fundamental for long term achievement. I always feel a little uncomfortable with the word entrepreneur. 'Oh, he's an entrepreneur! ... you know ... he's fast and furious'. Maybe it will work, maybe it won't work. That's not me. I'm a belt and braces man."

It's this caution and attention to detail that has kept Sir Jackie at the forefront as a global businessman.

"You can pose and tell everyone how good you are,
but when the flag drops you've got to deliver."

JOHN BOYLE

Hall of Fame | 1997

THANK YOU, JOHN BOYLE. You have been one of life's great enrichers. You understood more than anyone that holidays are precious to the working people of Scotland. Our weather is so awful and unpredictable that we needed two weeks in the scorching sunshine every year to recharge our weary bodies. You saw the absurd restrictions of the travel business and the monumental rip-offs. And your business, Direct Holidays, changed the way we took time off. Few people have the ability to make such an impact on life. You deserve a garland.

John Boyle's gregarious persona has permeated the cultural and business life of Scotland for 20 years.

"I think we are getting better at dealing with success in Scotland, but there is still a bit of jealousy and resentment in some quarters about people who have made a lot of money," he says.

He is an individual whose activities feature more in the tabloid and sports pages than on the business pages. He's been a major backer of Motherwell football club, so pleasure and pain have been meted out in equal measure. But John's resilience and boundless energy have seen him through.

There is a generosity of spirit and a surfeit of ideas. His company, Hamilton Portfolio, is a boutique investment company based in Glasgow. It has a successful track record with interests in property, the media and technology.

Excessive, maybe sometimes even vulnerable, he knows what he likes. He loves opera and country music. He hates the way Christmas has become a retail jungle, so he heads off to Australia. He battles with his fitness, cycling through Vietnam or Morocco to keep off the weight, raising thousands for charity at the same time.

"I'm interested in art and ideas. I'd rather read a book than go to the gym," he admits.

Referring to his high profile social circle, he says: "Some sections of the media think we sit up in Glasgow G12 and plot the future of Scotland. But we simply enjoy each others' company."

Direct Holidays changed consumer habits and gave financial backers a giant return on investment. Now his Canadian low-cost airline is the toast of the skies. Zoom has become a fixture in a fickle market where budget carriers come and go. But John and his brother Hugh are battle-hardened veterans of the travel trade and they will keep on flying the Atlantic.

"I believe in making life enjoyable and a bit of fun for the people who work with me. Look after your people and they will reciprocate. The travel business is exciting but it is demanding. It is people's holiday time and they want it to be right."

Motivation is a specialist subject for John. How does he do it? He takes his whole airline team on a chartered jet to Cuba for a party, all expenses paid. That's his style.

"I believe in making life enjoyable and a bit of fun for the people who work with me."

BRIAN SOUTER

Hall of Fame | 1998

THE STAGECOACH STORY has rolled along, often through hostile terrain. But Brian Souter and his sister Ann Gloag have proven they are Scotland's most resilient entrepreneurs. He's faced personal slings and arrows. He was ambushed by cowboys and vilified by some who failed to recognise his honesty and deep sincerity. Now Brian Souter prefers to keep his beady eye on the buses, trains and a portfolio of private investments.

Brian Souter is enigmatic: a Red Flag-waving socialist with a firm Christian faith who grabbed an opportunity when Conservative leader Margaret Thatcher deregulated the nationalised transport industry. "I'm basically a transport entrepreneur. That's what I've been immersed in and that's what I know best. We worked very hard to set up the business and it was tough, but we have always been committed to the idea of public transport and service to the customers. As entrepreneurs, Ann and I genuinely felt we could do it far better than the national bus services. I think we were absolutely right."

Today buses are safer, cleaner and more comfortable. In Scotland alone the number of people using buses has increased for six years in a row, with more than 465 million journeys recorded.

In his earlier days, Stagecoach was petulant and aggressive, storming ahead in every direction, criss-crossing the UK, then the world. Africa, Hong Kong, New Zealand were all part of the emerging empire. But Stagecoach was heading off in the wrong direction when it bought CoachUSA, a disparate and unwieldy American business. Stagecoach was a listed business and it was listing.

But Souter is an astute lateral thinker and faced up to his problems. He found his own solutions. Now he is an older and wiser entrepreneur. "I admit I took my foot off the gas. The business needed my focus and attention. I don't mind admitting that. I came back stronger, with the scars to prove it."

Much of this resolve was instilled as a Perth laddie cocooned by a close-knit working class household. His father was committed to his work, to the church and to making a few bob buying cars. "I didn't set out to make a lot of money. But having money brings an enormous amount of responsibility," he says.

He is cautious now after being dragged into the political limelight soon after the formation of the Scottish Parliament. "There's been a lot said about me in the past. I like to keep my values to myself. I don't want to abandon them but I'm not going to impose them on anyone."

"I'm happy to talk about my business. We're proud of the recent success of Megabus.com and Virgin Rail has changed the face of rail travel with hundreds of new trains."

The idiosyncrasies remain: his dog-tooth Tweed jacket with patched elbows, open-collar shirt and his Kickers. He often carries the company financial reports in a supermarket plastic bag.

What is the key to his success? "If I say anything it might sound very egocentric and trite. Providence has been good to us. It's been a journey for us. We've been in the right place at the right time and taken our opportunities. Simple as that."

"It's been a journey for us. We've been in the right place at the right time and taken our opportunities. Simple as that."

RICHARD EMANUEL MBE

Hall of Fame | 1999

THE WISEST PEOPLE CARVE OUT TIME for the serendipity of meetings with strangers. Often an unpromising engagement can turn out to be a mutually beneficial turning point. Richard Emanuel has always found time in his busy, well-ordered schedule for new thinking.

After all, he was a young guy in his early 20s when he contacted Sir Tom Farmer. The Kwik-Fit tycoon agreed to meet this unknown Glaswegian sharing with him a few pearls of wisdom and a contact or two.

"It was a great thing for Sir Tom to do. He was busy and successful and didn't need to see me. But he gave me his time and it was of great help. We kept in contact and he acted as my mentor as my business grew and became successful," says Richard, who has flown in to the Gleneagles Hotel for a business meeting.

Today Emanuel, now 38, is one of Scotland's wealthiest men under 40. With a thriving business, based in The Netherlands, serving Europe and Africa, a luxury home on the Cote d'Azur, and a repair factory in Scotland employing several hundred, he has won international plaudits and respect for his entrepreneurial achievements.

He has come a long way in a short time. He set up his business at 23 and recalls the faith of the Bank of Scotland manager at Newlands, who agreed to a £3,000 overdraft in 1991. This helped him create DX Communications and the Bank of Scotland has continued to be supportive ever since.

"The fundamentals of business don't really change. It's just the numbers get bigger. There are more zeros at the end now," says Richard. "I don't think you should spoon-feed people to become entrepreneurs. There's a natural selection process of hard knocks that you often need to go through to say 'I am really determined'. In my view, it's this persistence and the ability to overcome failure that breeds sustained success in business."

Although the son of varsity teachers, Richard wasn't keen on pursuing higher education. At six foot four, he was fit and active, dark-haired and good-looking. His first job was in a health and fitness club in Queen Street in Glasgow.

"I worked as a trainee manager and one of the guys came in with this bricklike object. I was curious. It was one of the early mobile phones. It was expensive and was very clunky. But it started me thinking."

So mobile phones would become his future. He approached a supplier and was given a brief opportunity to sell the phones. He went to see customers and started to shift a fair number. "I was very focused on two things: sales and customer service. I was very keen to extol the benefits of having a mobile phone."

In 1993 Chris Gorman and John Whyte, who also had a small telecoms business in Govan, joined forces with DX Communications. "I admired John because he was a determined guy. Everything was against him yet he wanted to start his own business. Chris was just a dynamo who worked every hour of the day." It was an explosive combination of complementary talents. The business was sold to BT Cellnet in 1999 for £42 million. And the lines have been busy ever since.

"There's a natural selection process of hard knocks that you often need to go through to say 'I am really determined'."

JIM McCOLL OBE

Hall of Fame | 1999

WHO WOULD BE THE IDEAL DINNER GUEST for Jim McColl? A glamorous movie star, a legendary football manager or an intrepid Antarctic explorer? All would be welcome for a lively exchange of views but perhaps Warren Buffett – the Sage of Omaha – would give Jim the most cerebral pleasure. Both men share the finely-tuned characteristics of the methodological, entrepreneurial investor.

Jim would be content to listen. He is still building a business matrix of considerable worth, value and longevity. His ambition is to create a Scottish business with market value of £1 billion. That's not empty braggadocio. Already his sound business sense makes this a highly attainable goal.

Like Buffett, Jim McColl deals with traditional investments that make obvious returns. His businesses clean power stations, remove the toxic waste, clean out the dangerous chemical cocktails and deal with the bulk wastes safely. It's a growing area, especially in China where the world's fastest-growing economy needs more coal-fired power stations to meet insatiable energy demands.

Jim's metier is to build teams, although his tasteful, wood-panelled head office in East Kilbride has fewer than 20 key people. His portfolio of companies includes Clyde Blowers, Clyde Bergemann, Clyde Material Handling, Clean Cut Technologies and Interbulk Investments. The Clyde brand is now well-known and respected in China, equal in the energy sector to General Electric or Siemens. "That's because we have been in there from the start."

While he remains his own man, he still studies Buffettology. And he quotes him: "We've read management theories that specify exactly how many managers should report to any one executive but they make little sense to us. When you have able managers of high character running businesses about which they are passionate, you can have a dozen or more reporting to you and still have time for an afternoon nap. Conversely if you have one person reporting to you who is deceitful, inept or uninterested, you will find yourself with more than you can handle."

He is proud of his south Lanarkshire working-class roots and his mother's influence in pushing him forward and building his self-confidence. "I am a believer in the power of education and how it can give you the tools to succeed. It's the basis for my success in business. I'm always learning something new."

He went to Strathclyde University, taking a new course, TBS, technology and business studies. He excelled and added an accountancy qualification, moving into business recovery and turning around a north-east oil services company. He bought into Clyde Blowers, but the growing business was misunderstood by the cloth-eared investment analysts. Mid-cap Scottish companies went out of favour on the London Stock Exchange and Jim McColl changed his strategy, taking the company private. Regrets? Too few to mention. Instead of Sinatra, it's the Sage again.

"Observing correctly that the market was frequently efficient, the proponents of finance theory went on to conclude, incorrectly, that it was always efficient. The difference between these propositions is night and day."

While the great doors of China are now swinging open for business, the Clyde companies are already in, up the stairs, in the front-room and having their jasmine tea. Jim McColl is ahead of the game and that's where he intends to stay for many years to come.

"I am a believer in the power of education and how it can give you the tools to succeed. It's the basis for my success in business. I'm always learning something new"

DAVID SIBBALD

Hall of Fame | 2000

CRY FREEDOM is an apposite rallying call for David Sibbald. It means freedom from poverty, human misery and illiteracy. His Kate MacAskill Foundation, named after his much-adored centenarian grandmother, is helping to educate and care for the less fortunate in Africa and Afghanistan. This is at the core of the Sibbald credo. In 1981, when he left university in Glasgow, he couldn't find a job. Norman Tebbit told the unemployed to: "Get On Your Bike". So David went off to work in South Africa. With girlfriend, Catriona, later his wife, he toured Namibia, Mozambique and Botswana in a battered VW Variant. They fell in love, with each other and with Africa.

David Sibbald is measured and cautious. As a software developer, he made his fortune in the thick of the dot.com boom in the late 1990s. Alan Greenspan's famous phrase for the technological bubble was "irrational exuberance". And it was. Vast fortunes were made; much more value was destroyed. Pension funds and investments took a battering. Trust was broken.

Sibbald worked in Silicon Valley and witnessed first hand the opportunities. But, driven by some invisible Calvinistic work ethic, he wanted to run his own show. He came home to Scotland and created Atlantech, an innovative software company, in 1992. It was a great business, with talented people. It was sold in 2000 to Cisco Systems for $180 million. "It was the right thing to do," he maintains. "We were a small player, we either had to borrow to make acquisitions or get taken over by a bigger business. Cisco Systems was an excellent deal."

For a while, Sibbald became a company man, caged like a noble African lion. He wanted his own freedom back. So he started again. He set up Sumerian Networks, an IT company with a memory. It remembers that promises about IT were made before and quickly broken. It has a memory of what not to do. "We are all a little bit older and a lot wiser," he says. "We don't make promises we can't deliver." Sumerian Networks sells no-nonsense expertise.

It is a Scottish-based business, growing incrementally, without haste or hype. "I don't want to return to those mad 14-hour days. I'm trying to get a better balance," he says.

"Honest, hard work is pretty important to the Scottish psyche and when substantial material gain is a consequence, then I believe you have to recycle this material wealth back to those less fortunate. There is only so much that any individual human being needs. I don't think conspicuous consumption is something we should celebrate when there are so many other people looking for a chance or an opportunity to realise their full potential."

This new business balance gives Sibbald more time to pursue his other passion: his work in Somalia where it's either hands-on working in the orphanage with Catriona, a trained midwife, and his family, or building homes in Kenya.

And while his knees still hold out, he turns out for his Renfrewshire vet's football team. He still has a passion for the Scottish game. Still has a dream that he might pull on the dark-blue Scotland jersey in the World Cup Final against the Auld Enemy. Sibbald knows the importance of dreams.

"Honest, hard work is pretty important to the Scottish psyche and when substantial material gain is a consequence, then I believe you have to recycle this material wealth back to those less fortunate."

SIR ARNOLD CLARK

Hall of Fame | 2000

SIR ARNOLD CLARK STILL CALLS IT THE MOTOR CAR.

No automobile affectations for Scotland's undisputed king of car sales. From Belisha beacons, to traffic lights and motorway bollards, Arnold Clark's moniker has been an integral part of the British motoring landscape for over 50 years. The democratisation of modern car ownership in Scotland runs parallel with his prolonged success.

After the Second World War, the former RAF mechanic started out in a landscape of petrol rationing and ownership restriction. In 1949, he was demobbed, married and had a baby son. His savings dwindled to £2 10/-. "I had to get working to support my family."

His work ethic was phenomenal. He'd leave home at 4am, drive to Elgin, then to Forres. He snapped up every second-hand car he could find, renovated it and sold it in Glasgow. Then he would do it again and again. He lived a frugal life on less than £10 a week and salted away all the rest. He continually reinvested.

"I've always said it is important to enjoy what you're doing in life and that's what I try to do in business."

He built a reputation for straight dealing. No tricks or dodges. He bought his first car showroom in 52 Park Road for £1200 and bought 40 second-hand cars, he sold half in the first week. He still owns the showroom.

By 1962, he'd opened a shiny showroom in the centre of Glasgow and three years later he had an empire worth £2 million. In 1965, *The Sunday Post* proclaimed: "He's only 37. He could retire tomorrow and live like a lord. But the best years are still ahead." The paper was spot-on.

"I decided to use my signature and my own name to give the business the personal touch. I still believe it means a lot to the customer." Arnold Clark continued to thrive to become one of the UK's largest privately owned businesses.

Arnold was an innovator. He pioneered the concept of after-sales service and hire purchase. From the start he had a scheme "a three month guarantee". It became his no quibble guarantee that instilled customer loyalty and repeat business. He was the agent for BMC cars, the Austin Cambridges and Morris Oxfords of yesteryear, then for Rootes and the Scottish-built Hillman Imp. But he was most proud of winning the Jaguar franchise.

He introduced his hire purchase operation in 1963. He even invented zero per cent finance. There's a sign in the head office. Welcome: "My simple philosophy is to offer genuine value for money and create high levels of customer service."

He has earned every plaudit, every award for a life of perpetual work. But his honour from the Queen at the Palace of Holyrood House gave him particular pleasure as a Scot. Arise Sir Arnold, a knight of the road.

"I've always said it is important to enjoy what you're doing in life and that's what I try to do in business."

WILLIE HAUGHEY OBE

Hall of Fame | 2000

SUCCESSFUL ENTREPRENEURS need a head for heights. And Willie Haughey has climbed as high up the ladder of success as anyone in Scotland. Glasgow's dramatic skyline is an epic setting for an entrepreneur who has turned his City Refrigeration business into one of the UK's most successful service engineering and construction groups.

From this multi-storey vantage point, Willie can point out the Gorbals, where he'd tumble out of bed at 5am to deliver milk, and once he'd finished his rounds, go on to chop up and sell bundles of firewood. He can also see Parkhead, the hallowed ground of his beloved football heroes, Celtic. He can look over to Cambuslang, the heart of his UK-wide operation.

The sweltering forges, soot-encrusted factories and mighty shipyards have now been replaced by contact centres, Italian designer emporia and night clubs, but it is a backdrop that excites this Glaswegian.

"I've done well out of life and I can see there are others who need help and a fair-and-square chance to lead decent and fulfilling lives. It's not rocket science, it's common decency. We have one rule in our business: we take care of people. And I want to help people who want to help themselves," he says.

Willie's promising football career was cut short by injury and he pushed himself into engineering. Willie was willing and bright, and trained as a cooling engineer. He was a quick learner and headed out to Dubai where he was given responsibility at an early age. It taught him resilience and how to run a business. It gave him an edge in an edgy environment.

On his return in 1985 he set up City Refrigeration with his wife Susan, keeping the hottest spots in the City supplied with cool beer.

"We believed in our ability. We'd work the hours to get the job done properly. So when we were given the opportunity to take on the big projects we were ready; we had learned how to deal with scaling up."

In 1990 they faced a decision about whether to expand at Cambuslang. Susan and Willie borrowed £30,000 in trepidation from Bank of Scotland at Shawlands. It was bold. They built new offices. There was no sales brochure or salesmen, simply word of mouth. The business prospered, moving out beyond the licensed trade.

There was a step change when City Refrigeration won a lucrative contract to fit out the freezer cabinets and chillers for Asda. They were good at it too. So they were asked to tender for the whole facilities management for the UK business. They took it on with aplomb.

In 2004 City Refrigeration Holdings was voted the fastest growing business in Europe – now employing 10,000 people – and when asked for his unique selling point he said: "I don't have one." Perhaps he was being facetious; he has three selling points: service, service and the delivery of that service.

Without doubt, Willie will leave an indelible impression on his birth place. He has high aspirations for the Dear Green Place. His own endeavours have given him the ability to influence and make changes. He is admired for his tenacity and his straightforward, can-do attitude.

"We have one rule in our business: we take care of people.
And I want to help people who want to help themselves."

ANN GLOAG OBE

Hall of Fame | 2001

ANN GLOAG TREASURES HER TIME AS A NURSE. She tended to the needs of patients as a theatre sister in a Perthshire hospital. But as her young family grew up she needed extra income. And a new career as an entrepreneur crept up on her.

"I can honestly say that throughout the 20 years I worked in the National Health Service, I loved my time as a nurse. Then we set up a part-time business and I loved that too."

Bigger things were brewing. In 1980 she jump-started a fledgling bus company called Stagecoach with her brother Brian Souter and she took to this with gusto. The next 26 years have been a compelling story of penny-pinching persistence to unimaginable riches. The bus group, which started with two coaches on the Aberdeen to London run, has become one of the UK's largest transport groups, with several railway franchises.

"I found it a difficult decision to give up nursing when I really enjoyed it but I also loved the buzz and excitement of this new bus business," she says.

Ann was always juggling commitments with the help of her mum and dad, Ian, a bus driver. "I could not have managed without them."

Her dad was always buying and selling cars in his spare time. "When I was a kid, my dad used to take us to the Gallowgate car mart in Glasgow. He was entrepreneurial, always buying and selling stuff." As the young Souters grew older he would share the risk on a car deal with his kids. "He was very fair. He always gave you your due percentage – never more than that."

Running buses was everything in her life. "You have to remember that the nationalised Scottish Bus Group had a monopoly. There was no such thing as customer service – it just didn't exist, so there was a huge opportunity for us."

The Stagecoach training ground was harsh, although a rat-infested garage on the banks of the River Tay eventually gave way to better facilities. Growth was fast and furious and city-to-city networks began to spread. Ann remained hands-on for seven years answering the phones and dealing with the expanding business.

"I wasn't thinking about living in a castle," she laughs, sitting in her baronial pile at Kinfauns. "I was just wondering how I was going to pay my diesel bill next month."

In 1987, total deregulation brought a new dimension. Opportunities opened up for local bus networks and Stagecoach was ready and able, setting up a depot in Glasgow. Stagecoach moved from a mom-and-pop bus company to a corporate-in-waiting, bringing in German double-deckers. Ann took on a wider human resources role.

"I believe the heart of our success was being right in there at the beginning. We were always first over the parapet and getting shot at. But we still believed we had the right philosophy. If you weren't competitive, you were dead. You had to fight in every sense of the word for survival. It was either your survival or theirs."

This is all part of the folklore now. Ann enjoys the fruits of this victorious battle. She still sits on the Stagecoach board but has many interests, including Mercy Ships, a charity taking surgeons and medical staff to tend the sick in Africa. She regularly helps out in theatre. But those early Perth memories are still very precious.

"If you weren't competitive, you were dead. You had to fight in every sense of the word for survival. It was either your survival or theirs."

SAM RUSSELL MBE

Hall of Fame | 2001

THE IRRESISTIBLE AROMA of a business deal still drives him. His group has evolved into a global operation providing manufacturing solutions to almost every business sector. But Sam Russell, the founder of the Simclar Group, remains motivated by the need to be fleet-of-foot, by continually moving up the value-chain. It's why he keeps going. He hasn't lost one iota of his determination and drive and still has a desire to make Simclar Group a recognised global brand with turnover upwards of $500 million.

He's a quietly-spoken, very likeable person. A gentleman indeed. A map on his office wall pinpoints seven operations across the United States, one in Mexico and two in China. You can count on one hand the Scottish companies listed on NASDAQ, America's second stock exchange. Simclar's US subsidiary is one of these companies.

By 2001, its 25th anniversary, Simclar employed 900 people and had a turnover of £70 million. But leaner times were ahead. Manufacturing in low cost countries became necessary for survival in Scotland. Tough decisions were made: jobs were lost to protect the core activities.

"I love Scotland, but people have to understand that we are competing globally. We have to manufacture abroad, but keep the ideas and the design – the high-value product – here."

Scottish prudence allowed Simclar to move ahead again, in 2001 buying a majority stake in Techdyne, a US corporation with manufacturing facilities in Florida, Ohio, Massachusetts and Texas. This was followed, in 2002, by the purchase of Fullarton, another Scottish company, but with factories also in Texas, North Carolina and China. In 2003, Simclar purchased AG Technologies, with a manufacturing plant in Mexico, and in 2005 bought UP Mex, a seating components business based in Lancashire. Most recently, in early 2006, Simclar purchased Litton Interconnect Technologies with facilities in Fife, Missouri and China.

Today Simclar employs around 2,500 people worldwide.

A Jedburgh Callant in 1965, Sam played both rugby and football and started his working life as the first apprentice toolmaker with L.S. Starrett Co. He moved to work in Fife with US-owned Varian, as a jig-tool draftsman, and went to night school to gain an HNC in mechanical engineering and a diploma in industrial management.

Sam moved to Bourns Trimpot and then to W.L. Gore, which manufactured cables for the burgeoning computer industry. Sam had immense admiration for the founders, Bill and Vieve Gore, and worked closely with their son, Bob, in the business in Dunfermline. "This gave me invaluable experience."

He set up Simclar in 1976 using a braiding machine to screen harnesses for IBM. "I always had the desire to set up in business and so with £140 investment started in my garage at home. It was a risk. I worked the first six months without a salary."

Sam admires the "can-do" attitude of Americans. "Too often in the UK we say we can't do this because of some spurious reason. I always ask: 'What can you do to make this work?' I like to talk about turning the stone, looking at the problem and asking 'what if?'"

He remains a private family man, supported by his wife Christina, his son Simon, who is handicapped, and his daughter Clara, a medical doctor.

"I like to talk about turning the stone, looking at the problem and asking 'what if?'"

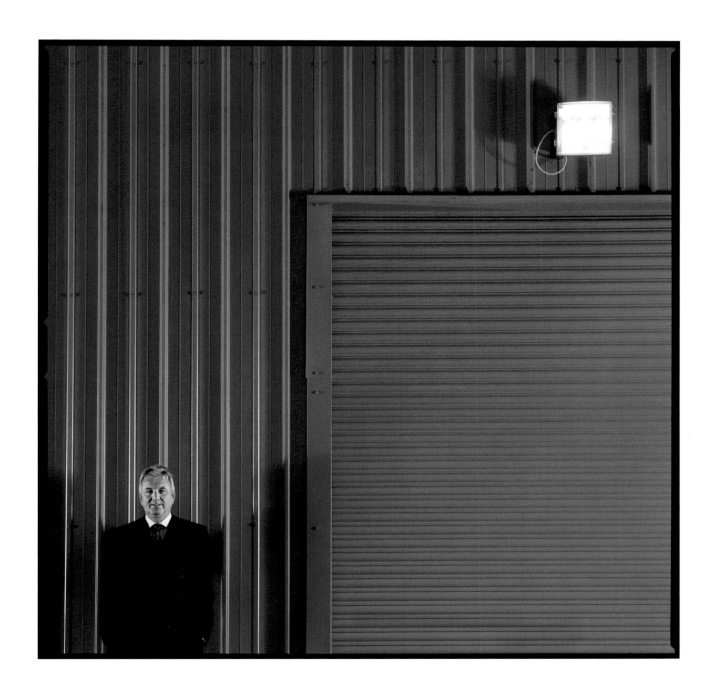

SIR IAN WOOD CBE

Hall of Fame | 2002

A GATHERING OF DISTINGUISHED BUSINESSMEN and their bankers were indulging in a post-prandial game in the dining room of the New Club in Edinburgh. "So how many Scottish companies can be said to be truly global," posed one gentleman.

It was an interesting parlour game. If you remove the whisky and drinks business it was hard to find a Scottish company with tentacles in every continent. Names on the table were the Weir Group, Aggreko, Clyde Blowers. But the verdict. "It has to be the Wood Group"

And it was agreed that the Aberdeen-based energy services company, listed on the London Stock Market in 2002, was a truly international business. Each local business has been able to retain its distinctive identity, from the Copgo Wood Group in Argentina, to JP Kenny, the subsea and pipeline engineering business, to the global deepwater engineering business, Mustang. The Group's work spans North America, Venezuela, Brazil, North and West Africa, Russia, India, China, the Middle East and Asia Pacific. All owned and overseen by the Wood Group.

Of all the entrepreneurs in Scotland, Sir Ian Wood has created an international business with carbon footprints in every continent. Sir Ian has the air of an incisive academic, a thinker and planner. He is parsimonious without being mean. He trained as a psychologist, not an engineer. He took over his father's trawling business and redefined it in the early 1970s as a support services business for oil & gas. He knitted these skills well when he was chair of Scottish Enterprise.

"My whole job is people. I can't design an engine. I have to bet on the best people. I'm not like Andy Grove at Intel; he knows how to make a chip. I'm more of a coach. I'll get involved in strategic decisions such as acquisitions and I thrive on creating great teams and giving them the self-confidence to do their job. That's our success."

This explains a great deal. Sir Ian's business bible is the best-selling business book: *Good To Great* by entrepreneurial guru Jim Collins. The book's principal theme strikes a resonant chord with this thoughtful Granite City business figure. It says: "To go from good to great requires transcending the curse of competence. Just because something is your core business does not necessarily mean you can be the best in the world."

Wood Group is a serious, heavy-duty company working in ultra-extreme environments, where assets are hugely expensive, components need to be robust, and people kept safe. "Our business operates in the harshest conditions that the elements can throw at us. We all need to work together effectively to combat the daily challenges," he says.

Jim Collins talks about Level Five leadership. How reserved and self-effacing leaders build enduring greatness through a paradoxical blend of personal humility and professional will. Such leaders channel their egos away from themselves and into a larger goal of building a great company. If Scotland has any Level Five leaders – and they are rare – then Sir Ian Wood is probably the nearest to the real thing.

"My whole job is people. I can't design an engine. I have to bet on the best people … I thrive on creating great teams and giving them the self-confidence to do their job."

DONALD MACDONALD OBE

Hall of Fame | 2002

THE PUNGENT SCENT OF PEAT IN THE HEARTH and home-made

barley broth simmering on the stove. It's a cosy memory of an industrious Hebridean household woven like Harris Tweed through the life of Donald Macdonald. It conjures up a simple, often hard, but uncomplicated life on a croft. "There was a tremendous sense of self-sufficiency. People shared what they had," recalls Donald. "My mother was horrified when I told her I was going into the hotel trade."

When Donald started his career with British Transport Hotels, at Turnberry, he wasn't destined to become an entrepreneur. Yet Macdonald Hotels is one of the largest independent hotel groups in the UK with over 60 hotels. The Bathgate-based group owns some fine country hotels: the Randolph in Oxford, the Bath Spa, the Compleat Angler at Marlow and Ardoe House in Aberdeen but he has a soft spot for Aviemore, and the regeneration of the Highland resort.

Donald is a reserved Islander, not flamboyant or ostentatious. Some might call him dour, yet it is more likely to be his strong Christian faith you see. Proverbs 22 is his epithet: 'A good name is more desirable than great riches'. Perhaps Romans 12:10 is also appropriate: 'Practise hospitality'. For warmed up and settled back, he is a gracious host.

He talks about the "emotional" potential of the tourism experience in Britain and the need to embrace the kind of five-star service culture prevalent in other nations: Switzerland, Canada and the South of Ireland.

His favourite analogy is a three-legged stool, a suitable piece of furniture for the uneven stone floor of the croft. "There are three key elements to our business; people, product, and profits. It's a three-legged stool and it becomes uncomfortable if you allow one leg to become shorter than the other two."

Donald worked with Reo Stakis, the famed Cypriot hotelier who brought prawn cocktails, steak and chips, Black Forest gateau – and the roulette wheel – to a post-war generation of Scots. He spent 21 years with Stakis, and worked alongside Ken McCulloch, the Malmaison boutique hotel visionary. Then Donald made the decision to go on his own when Stakis sacrificed its main board executives to give the Founder's son an obstruction free path going forward. "I was 42 and, while I was comfortable, I was far too young to retire." he says. "I don't really see myself as a classic entrepreneur. I was in my forties when we set up the hotel group. I view myself more as a business person," he says modestly.

After six highly successful years, he was encouraged to go for a listing on the London Stock Exchange. He was given tremendous encouragement from the Bank of Scotland who became stalwart investors. But the London Stock Market was unappetising. The stool legs became too shaky. Donald found 80% of his time was spent trying to please unyielding City investors – all at the expense of his service ethos.

"It wasn't right for us. We are in a long-term business. The Stock Market encouraged us to focus on short-term decisions to improve year-on-year profits. In our business it doesn't work like this. The fabric and quality of hotels suffered as well as the development of our staff and executives".

Macdonald Hotels became privately-owned again in 2003 in the biggest Scottish public to private buyout to that date, backed by Peter Cummings of the Bank of Scotland. The stool was back in balance. "I can't say I'm an ambitious person. What I've done is as a result of a low boredom threshold leading to seeking fresh challenges."

> *"There are three key elements to our business; people, the product, and the profits.*
> *It's a three-legged stool and it becomes unbalanced if you take one leg away."*

MOIR LOCKHEAD OBE

Hall of Fame | 2002

FIRST IMPRESSIONS ARE DECEPTIVE. Moir Lockhead appears dour, dark and fierce seated beside his expansive desk with its tidy piles of paper and pamphlets. But when asked for a sound bite about his business, a smile lights up his whole face.

"I'm very proud of what we have achieved. We are the largest UK-listed surface transport group with buses and trains. We have annual revenues of more than £3 billion, with a market capitalisation of £1.6 billion." Add to this their extensive overseas business in North America, which includes over 20,000 yellow school buses, a transit management and contracting business and an expanding services division. And, of course, First ScotRail passenger rail franchise in Scotland.

All this from a municipal bus group freed from public shackles in the early 1980s. It is a formidable achievement for a miner's grandson who started out as a humble bus mechanic.

Now it's a quirk of fate that Britain's largest transport group should be based in Aberdeen. Moir Lockhead, born in a mining village in the county of Durham, has become an adopted Scot. He loves Aberdeenshire. His leisure time is spent helping his wife and daughter raise cattle on the rich farmland at Torphins, on Royal Deeside, with its majestic sweep towards Lochnagar.

But the transport business has been his calling. He headed north to Glasgow as the Chief Engineer on the Underground. It was the year the Clockwork Orange was reopened by the Queen. Later he arrived in the Granite City as head of Grampian Bus Group, but he could see the fast approaching opportunities of privatisation. Aided by some shrewd local investors and advisers, he grabbed his opportunity. Grampian was in the vanguard of the Thatcherite revolution which privatised the bus industry, then British Rail. An epoch of change was plotted in Aberdeen when a merger of Badgerline and Grampian created FirstBus in 1995.

He is not a fussy man. "I like to keep things simple. I like our people to be smart and presentable. I like our buses and trains to be clean and on time. Instructions should be clear and simple. I want to make public transport simpler and easy to use. That's why we have more colour coding and clearer information for the traveller.

"Transport groups require a lot of people and they are working to serve the general public. It is a labour intensive business. You need drivers and ticket collectors, mechanics and cleaners. First Group employs more than 70,000 people, split roughly 50-50 between the UK and North America. That's a lot to look after."

Every day three million passengers flick their passes or stump up money on one of 9,300 buses in the UK. Now they want greener buses with less emissions and Moir is committed to this too.

He isn't a big shot. "I don't see myself as an entrepreneur in the classic mould. I'm really a manager who works to pull together good teams. That's our strength. First Group has some extremely talented people leading our teams. When we started out, some of the people were very young and they have stayed with the business and now they are mature and experienced managers with a wealth of knowledge. That's been the key for us, I believe.

"Yes, there is a lot of travelling but I am happy to get home. I think the north-east of Scotland is one of the safest and best places in the world. You can try and knock Scotland but as a nation we have a huge amount going for us."

"I like to keep things simple. I like our people to be smart and presentable.
I like our buses and trains to be clean and on time."

CHRIS GORMAN OBE

Hall of Fame | 2003

LADIES AND GENTLEMEN, the star of tonight's show is …. Chris Gorman. He is a loquacious party-machine who divides opinion. Some snipers say he is an exhibitionist who struck it lucky. Others a butterfly fluttering on the petals of popular culture. Yet Chris – in spite of his media persona and reputation for throwing memorable parties – has been largely misunderstood.

He is an immensely generous and open individual who has shared his success with friends and family. While he might have worn his heart on his sleeve, he has an uncanny ability to communicate. He is a catalystic entrepreneur with the common touch.

"I'm good at inspiring people to achieve things they didn't think possible," he says. "I enjoy the challenge of taking an idea and then turning it into something real that makes money. And I want to help other people realise this ambition too."

He's experienced turbulent times, including the high profile collapse of Gadget Shop. But he remains undeterred, keeping up his high-energy lifestyle and passing on his own nuggets about the route to success.

"There's nothing wrong with failure. You learn far more about yourself and what you are capable of achieving if you've gone through something traumatic," he says.

A personal triumph involves his love of music. He organised the Live8 rock and pop concert in Scotland for the Make Poverty History campaign in July 2005. He was warned that something of this magnitude couldn't be organised in six weeks. This a personal challenge. He pulled in favours, cajoled and charmed. But 68,000 crammed in to Murrayfield stadium for an unforgettable evening.

Music remains a central theme and he spends hours in his private recording studio with friends and family. "It kept me out of trouble at school when I played the cello in the school orchestra."

He played drums in a band, Silent Witness, and organised delivery boys in a paper shop in Hartlepool, taking over the milk rounds and learning about the merits of customer service. He worked very hard and created his breaks, making his first millions with DX Communications, a mobile phone business. He repeated it with Reality and has since invested in a host of other ideas. He became a TV celebrity on Channel 4's *Make Me A Million*, helping two young entrepreneurs launch their diet business. He has also been playing his aces with the creation of Purple Lounge, an online poker site with typical Gorman pizazz.

He loves having friends round to his comfortable Bridge of Weir mansion with its swimming pool, games room and bar. "When I've finished working I switch into social mode, and I put the same amount of energy into organising our house parties and social events or family activities with our four children. I can't help it," he says.

Mary, his wife and confidante, shelters Chris when he needs some space. And, like many entrepreneurs, he feels guilty when he steals some time for himself, off to his private cinema to watch The West Wing.

Whether it is addressing the Scottish Parliament on business issues, encouraging budding entrepreneurs in Scottish schools, or as visiting professor of entrepreneurship at University of Paisley, he gives his all – and with a generous heart. That alone makes Chris Gorman worth knowing.

"I enjoy the challenge of taking an idea
and then turning it into something real that makes money."

ALASDAIR LOCKE

Hall of Fame | 2003

THE OIL INDUSTRY IS NOTORIOUSLY CYCLICAL. The peaks and

troughs are as rough as the North Sea in February. But Alasdair Locke has built an exceptional business which is now a world leader in drilling for oil and gas. Increasingly precious commodities.

"Oil and gas are found in awkward places. You can't have a risk-less exploration environment. But you can avoid danger by being sensible and by calculating everything and ensuring detailed risk assessment," he says, speaking in his Aberdeen office. "All that a creative entrepreneur does is try and eliminate the risks. It's wrong to think we are all gung-ho gamblers."

Alasdair Locke, Executive Chairman of Abbot Group, bought KCA Deutag which owns and runs 30 offshore platforms in the North Sea, the Caspian Sea, Angola, and Sakhalin, off Japan. The business also owns and operates the North Sea's only modular drilling and well work-over rig. But it is not confined to offshore drilling and has a fleet of more than 50 land rigs, with more under construction for clients in Libya, Brunei, and Siberia.

Having acquired KCA in 1992 he turned a £27 million a year turnover Group with a loss of £3 million into a Group with a £4 million profit. "It had to be sorted out quickly and that was my main thrust from day one. I kept a close eye on the cash flow and the costs."

The business employs 5,000 people around the globe with the headquarters in Aberdeen. "You have to delegate and trust people."

Alasdair's mother was Scottish and his dad was a British Army brigadier. He was schooled in Perthshire and retains the demeanour of a businessman meticulously planning his campaign, marshalling forces and passing orders down the line. He studied history and economics at Oxford and took the traditional path to a job in the City of London. But he veered off to work for a large American bank in its oil and shipping finance division. He discovered a fascination with shipping and the global energy business. "Fairly early in life I discovered I was not cut out to work in big corporations. I knew I wanted to run my own business and be in charge of my own destiny," he admits.

By 29, he moved out to the Far East, working in Singapore as an investment specialist. He started his own businesses which later became the Abbot Group with its biggest prize, KCA Deutag. "In the late 1980s I could see that there was going to be intense consolidation in the North Sea. For the energy giants, in a mature market, drilling was no longer a core activity. I realised that outsourcing was the way ahead. It was eat or be eaten. All I did was to go out and recruit the best guys I could get. And they were all good because they had been trained by the oil giants."

His ambition remains: to create a sustainable global drilling company.

"Salesmanship is critical. All life is about making the sales pitch. Everyone within a business has to persuade people what they are doing is the right thing. To succeed you must have a clear vision – a focus on what you want to do and how you can do it. It's never been my intention to sell out. I wanted to be more than a deal-doer, I wanted to build a sustainable business."

Locke accepts at times it is a lonely vigil. "You are on your own and part of a team but the leadership and the buck stops with the man at the top."

"All that a creative entrepreneur does is try and eliminate the risks.
It's wrong to think we are all gung-ho gamblers."

WALTER NIMMO

Hall of Fame | 2003

PROFESSOR WALTER NIMMO could easily have pursued a career as a virtuoso musician, gracing the concert halls of the world. Instead, the Whitburn boy was drawn to medicine, university teaching and research, and eventually to business where he set up Inveresk Clinical Research.

A friend heaps paeans of praise on his multifarious talent. "He's a genius. A true polymath. A maestro even!" He explains: "We were out in New York securing the deal to sell Inveresk Research to the American firm Charles River Laboratories. Walter was an adroit negotiator, managing the delicate discussions. He got exactly what he wanted – and more. Later, when we were celebrating in a late-night Manhattan nightclub, Walter ended up at the piano playing breathtakingly brilliant jazz. An admiring crowd just lapped it up."

More than that: on a previous trip to Canada, he was called upon to deliver – successfully – a baby on the trans-atlantic flight when a passenger went into premature labour.

How does he do it? Life and work have been tremendously fulfilling for Walter Nimmo. He was a distinguished professor of anaesthetics at Sheffield University when another chapter opened. On 1st November 1988, he returned to Edinburgh to run a business. The next 16 years were a roller-coaster ride with Nimmo in the front carriage.

"It was a safe and secure job being a professor but I decided I wanted to take a risk and become more entrepreneurial. It was a calculated gamble but I've certainly enjoyed it."

"At first, it took four or five years to get Inveresk Clinical Research going, we succeeded by concentrating on our clients and ensuring our people were well looked after. But the United States increasingly became our focus. We needed a presence there because that was where most of the major drug testing was based."

Inveresk Research became acknowledged leaders in clinical research and testing, working for the major global pharmaceutical companies. They were snapped up by a Swiss company in 1993 but Nimmo stayed on and grew the combined businesses. Then he led a management buy-out and arranged a placing on NASDAQ.

"I've done the full range from start-up, selling out to an international listed company, merging the new business, taking it public, then reselling it. We didn't expect to make any money," he says with a broad smile. But they did. Nearly $1.5 billion. "We did well because we empowered our people, they were given more accountability for the profit and loss of their divisions. And they were rewarded too."

The Nimmo roller-coaster came to a halt in October 2004 when Charles River Laboratories stepped in. The new business is now a global leader in research models and services, at the forefront of drug safety testing and clinical development services. James Foster, its Chairman and CEO, was *Forbes* Magazine Entrepreneur of the Year in 2002. Professor Nimmo stayed for a while as scientific director, but he preferred his freedom. There were no regrets. Now he assists as an angel investor and his many other interests include a seat on the board of the Royal Scottish National Orchestra. For this professor, there's still time to fit in another action-packed career.

"We did well because we empowered our people, they were given more accountability for the profit and loss of their divisions. And they were rewarded too."

KEITH MILLER CBE

Hall of Fame | 2004

CAPITAL AND DEVELOPMENT. And even developments in the Capital. Keith Miller changes landscapes. Each year his business builds thousands of modern monuments across the UK where people live their daily lives.

But there's much more. The Miller Group is the UK's largest, privately-owned house-building, property development and construction business, now with interests stretched across Europe. And, under Keith Miller's direction, the group has recorded profit increases over 12 successive years, making significant acquisitions in England.

Keith Miller is modest, unfailingly polite and self-effacing. "I've never viewed myself as an entrepreneur. In my view, a true entrepreneur is someone, such as Brian Souter of Stagecoach, who has seen a gap in the market and set up something from scratch," he says.

Underneath this exterior, Miller is a ferocious competitor, who has scaled vertiginous Alpine peaks and raced in some of yachting's most treacherous ocean challenges. He admires sporting achievers: his business backs Olympic Gold Medal cyclist Chris Hoy and Scotland's greatest Olympian, the yachtswoman Shirley Robertson. While he admires their individual determination, he remains a team player.

"I always think it is matter of doing the best with the cards that you're dealt with in life. The number one priority for me in business is to surround myself with good people and to build excellent teams."

Armed with an honours degree in building from Heriot-Watt University and a Glasgow University management diploma, he joined the family business in 1975. His inspirational uncle was Sir James Miller, a co-founder in the 1930s, who became Lord Provost of Edinburgh and Lord Mayor of London. Young Keith worked in the mining division and in 1976, aged 27, he was appointed board director with responsibility for coal mining activities in the UK and the US. A decade later, he earned promotion to become Managing Director of Miller Developments, responsible for the commercial property development and investment division.

He was appointed Chief Executive in 1994 and has since changed the face of Miller Group. His achievements are the steady expansion of the businesses, making profits but increasing emphasis on customer satisfaction. The kind of modern homes we live in matters deeply to Keith Miller.

"Our whole approach has been to customer care. The experience of buying a house from us has to be at the highest level. I'm very proud that the surveys of existing customers show 85% would firmly recommend a Miller home – that was up from 50% in 2000. We're committed to this culture of quality."

But he has left his indelible mark on the public realm. He's co-chairman of New Edinburgh Ltd, a joint venture with the City's Council, which developed the prestigious Edinburgh Park, now home to the Miller Group itself. From his office overlooking the capital's bypass, he can view the continuing economic vibrancy of West Edinburgh – still very much a focus of his ambitions.

In January 2005 he was awarded the CBE for Services to the Construction Industry in Scotland and for his considerable work for charity. Keith lives in Edinburgh, a place he loves dearly, and is married with three daughters.

"The number one priority for me in business is to surround myself with good people and to build excellent teams."

GORDON BAXTER

Hall of Fame | 2004

GORDON BAXTER HAD ONE DRIVING AMBITION. To help his

parents build their business. As a young Morayshire lad he was smitten by the emerging science of biochemistry. After his first two years at Aberdeen University, he seriously considered devoting his life to help find a cure for cancer. But the war intervened and, instead, he returned to the family business, set up as a grocer's shop in Fochabers on Speyside in 1868, and built up Baxters, Scotland's best loved soup and quality food brand. Life's like that.

It is a fascinating story of perseverance, foresight and reward. Some might argue Gordon Baxter's commitment to wholesome comestibles in tins has done more to ward off ill health than a life looking down a microscope. He was a research chemist with the mighty ICI working on weapons development during the war. "It taught me how not to run a business. It was an us-and-them type of place where the management ordered you what to do." Communications with staff were poor.

So when he returned to the family business in 1946, with its modest turnover of £40,000 a year and 11 staff, including Gordon and his brother, he had major aspirations. "It took us 16 years to make our first million pounds in sales. This was in 1963. In 1975 this was up to £4 million and by 2000 that was £50 million." The business now has sales of more than £100 million a year with Gordon's daughter, Audrey, at the helm and her signature on the tins and packets. "I'm very proud of her. She is an outstanding Scottish business woman in her own right."

Gordon dubs Baxters' early years the Age of Innocence, followed by the Age of Slavery and, as the sales graph rose steadily, the Age of Enlightenment. With the help of his charming wife, Ena, who became a UK television celebrity for her cooking programmes, Baxters prospered. The business remained true to its principles: Quality is first, second and third (indeed Ena dumped monosodium glutamate and banned all artificial preservatives and colourings). "My mantra was simple: be different and better, embrace change and watch the cash flow," says Gordon.

The major names queued up to take-over the business: Heinz, Crosse & Blackwell, Campbell's and General Mills. In all, 189 take-over approaches – a possible *Guinness Book of Records* entry – but Gordon has politely resisted them all.

"What changed our lives was going to America in 1959. You saw this wonderful consumer market with vast emporia laden with merchandise we'd never seen in Britain. Poor old Britain, we weren't long out of coupons and rationing." Baxters was nothing in this cornucopia of consumer choice. He met a Chicago supermarket chief who put him straight. "Your products are good, but first you must find out what the American customer wants, make it and bring it to me. I'll sell it and I'll give you feet of shelf space."

"I realised the customer would not buy our products unless we made them well known and available. This meant marketing, advertising and all the things you do to build a modern brand. We came back to Scotland inspired. Instead of making what my granny had made we looked at what the consumer wanted. We changed our thinking. We learned: 'You innovate or you die'."

With Gordon, Ena and his brother, Ian, in charge of production and a willing band of helpers, the Baxter's business grew to become Britain's brand leaders in quality soups, beetroot and much more – all from a Speyside base. Gordon stepped back in 2000 and is now Life President, spending more time fishing for salmon on his beloved Spey, enjoying his family and friends and watching cricket round the world. Meanwhile Baxters is well and truly cooking.

"My mantra was simple: be different and better, embrace
change and watch the cash flow."

SIR BILL GAMMELL

Hall of Fame | 2005

BILL GAMMELL ALWAYS HAD MUCH TO PROVE. Some will point and say he was fortunate because his father, Jimmy Gammell, the doyen of Edinburgh's Charlotte Square, was a distinguished business tycoon: rich, cultured and a smart investor.

Yet Bill's achievements as a Scottish entrepreneur are exceptional by any standards. He has surpassed even his father's crowning achievements. He learned early lessons about being a winner playing rugby and earning several caps for Scotland. For many years, Bill Gammell's oil exploration company, Cairn Energy, was a minnow, a mere pinprick in the side of the giant players. Yes, he was known for his impeccable political connections, a boyhood friend of both George Bush and Tony Blair, but Cairn was not globally significant.

But Bill's dogged entrepreneurial persistence paid dividends. In January 2005, Cairn Energy announced a major oil find in India – and within weeks the stock had catapulted his company onto the FTSE 100 giving the company a market capital of £3 billion – making it one of the top five companies in Scotland.

"I think an entrepreneur is all about being brave and bold. And not being at all frightened to be a contrarian. Any businessman or entrepreneur needs three things: they've got to have a strong vision, they've got to be very focused, and they've got to have some particular competitive business edge," he explains sitting in his Edinburgh boardroom, with its stunning views of the Castle.

"We say vision without action is a daydream: but action without vision is a nightmare. And I think it is the job of the entrepreneur or the leader to be the catalyst to transform the vision into action."

For Bill, the entrepreneur must be prepared to transform vision into action. "A lot of people would like to take responsibility, very few do because they have an aversion to risk ... they have a fear of failure. And failure is only a lesson on the way to success."

But Cairn Energy is a teamwork story; with oil-field engineers, drillers, seismic experts and geologists. "I think it is hugely important that entrepreneurs surround themselves with a lot of very capable people. One of the few talents I have is the ability to employ people who are brighter than me. I encourage other people to hire those who are better than themselves in some way. I want to know how we can get something done, not all the reasons to stop something happening."

Bill's ingredients for success require a sharp measure of humility and reality, coupled with determination.

"If you believe strongly enough that a particular course of action is the way to go you must persuade your team to be supportive of you or, if necessary, change the team. You must have a team of people working together. That's what a team stands for in my view. Together everyone achieves more."

But there is something a little extra. Bill's core belief is that any high-energy team must also have a real desire to push themselves beyond their comfort zone to achieve things that they did not believe were within their grasp. That's the Gammell way.

"We say vision without action is a daydream:
but action without vision is a nightmare."

WORDS OF INSPIRATION

Many successful entrepreneurs have served on the board of The Entrepreneurial Exchange over the years. Here is a selection of Words of Inspiration from them.

"Manage your personal reputation the way you manage your business – carefully and continually"
Alastair Balfour (1995 to 1998; 2001 to 2004)

"Be focused, be ambitious and be honest. Recruit and empower a team of excellent people with complementary skills that will be dedicated to achieving agreed objectives.
Gordon Barraclough (1999 to 2002)

"Entrepreneurs are always coming up with great business ideas but success will not come unless you surround yourself with great people at the top."
Gordon Beattie (1998 to 2002)

"Create products or services that are unique and different from your competitors. If you don't, all you have is price."
Gio Benedetti (1997 to 2003)

"Keep a clear head, take good risks, look after your people and be prepared to work very hard."
Norma Corlette (2005 to date)

"Accept that you will make mistakes but be proud of the fact that you are strong enough to recognise them, learn from them and use the knowledge to improve your business going forward."
Simon Coyle (2004 to 2005)

"Those who think a thing is impossible should not interrupt those that are doing it."
Robin Dunseath (1997 to 1999)

"No amount of genius can overcome a preoccupation with detail."
Bill Fleming (2001 to 2005)

"It takes years of hard work to become an overnight success. Be prepared to put in the long hours and make lots of personal sacrifices. Try not to let emotions get in the way when making the tough decisions …welcome to the world of the entrepreneur!"
Charan Gill, MBE (2002 to date)

"Aspiring to create a great business will absorb your life, and the lives of those close to you. Ensure this commitment is meaningful. It's not just about trying to make money – it's about leaving the world a better place."
Nelson Gray (2002 to date)

"Enjoy what you do and the focus will be there."
Professor Russel Griggs (1996 to 1999)

"You don't need a lot. Just drive, organisation, tenacity, passion, self-belief, long hours... oh, and some luck!"
Professor Ron Lander OBE (1995 to 1998)

"Build "fabulous" teams who fight the right battles with integrity and honesty and have fun doing so."
Alison Loudon (2000 to date)

"Success comes from building the best teams and then looking after them"
Alan McCafferty (2004 to date)

"Get networking. In business and in life you can never have too many friends. Make it your ambition to get to anyone you need to with one phone call!"
John McGlynn (2004 to date)

"Understand your business, and that of your competitors, down to the last detail. Don't be afraid of risk but listen to advice before making the final decision."
James Milne (2004 to date)

"If we can be first to take the blame, then we find out what went wrong a lot quicker, with more clarity, and find a more direct route to putting it right – or making sure it doesn't happen again."
John Morgan (1996 to 2002; 2003 to date)

"Always write down your key objectives – and attach a time line to them. There is something about putting your goals down on paper that makes them more likely to happen."
Angela Paterson (2003 to date)

"The development of an innovation into a business success demands focus and dedication to a level verging upon fanaticism, where the business goal envelopes the entrepreneur to the exclusion of all else."
Andrew Reid (1998 to 2001)

"Seize opportunities – don't put off till tomorrow what you can do today."
Ann Rushforth, MBE (1999 to date)

"Be original, be inventive, be constructive not destructive have the drive and ambition to make your journey a dream. Go for it and never regret it."
Rita Rusk (1996 to 2000)

"Work hard, play hard."
Mike Rutterford (2002 to 2005)

"Do it now. You become successful the moment you start moving towards achieving your goals"
Iain Stirling (2005 to date)

"Follow your instincts, do not take things at face value, stick to the business you know best. The best deal may be the one you never did."
Donald Storrie (1995 to 1999)

"The only difference between people who succeed and people who don't is an ability to overcome unforeseeable obstacles".
Gerald Weisfeld (1995 to 1996)

"If you want to manage your business then control your cash. If you want someone else to control your business then don't manage your cash"
Brian Williamson (2005 to date)

MEMBERS OF THE ENTREPRENEURIAL EXCHANGE
1 MAY 2006

Gordon Adam
Head Resourcing

David Adams
Adams Consulting Group Ltd

Brian Aitchison
Levern Towers Ventures

Steven Alexander
Echelon Wealth Management

Keith Anderson
Boston Networks Ltd

James Anderson
Fresh Tan Ltd

James Andrew
Morris & Spottiswood Ltd

Roderick Angus
Merson Signs Ltd

Paul Atkinson
Head Resourcing

Richard Bailey
Atesta Group Ltd

Alastair Balfour
2in10 Ltd

Sharon Bamford
Scottish Institute for Enterprise

James Barnes
Dobbies Garden Centres plc

Andrew Barton
Recruitment Zone Ltd

Callum Bastock
Consolidated Carriers Ltd

Gordon Baxter
Baxters Food Group

Gordon Beattie
Beattie Communications Ltd

Max Beck
Land Locator Company

Martin Bell
Castle View International Holdings
Ltd

Gio Benedetti
Benedetti International plc

Greg Benson
Martin Groundland & Co Ltd

Stewart Binnie-McKenzie
Neilson Binnie McKenzie Ltd

Jim Bishop
Ernst & Young.

Scott Black
Finlayson Wagner Black Ltd

Jamie Black
Fusion Hair Nails & Beauty

Jack Black
MindStore

Colin Blair
Buzzworks Group

Kenny Blair
Buzzworks Group

Joseph Blake
Coltas Ltd

Frank Blin
PricewaterhouseCoopers

John Boyle
The Hamilton Portfolio Ltd

Amanda Boyle
Caledonia Contracts Ltd

Jackie Brierton
Scotcom Media Monitoring

Caroline Briggs
Amici Procurement Solutions

David Buchanan
Logical Innovations Ltd

Graham Bucknall
Adventi Ltd

David Budge
Budge PR Ltd

Alison Burns
P3 Music Ltd

Donna Burns
Passionara Ltd

James Butchart
Response Property Maintenance Ltd

Lynne Cadenhead
1745 Trading Company Ltd

Pamela Caira
BIG Partnership

Colin Aitken
UBS AG Private Banking

Gordon Cairns
Cairns Bond Ltd

Graham Callander
CMCR

Duncan Campbell
Zygomatics Ltd

Gordon Campbell
Dynamic Concepts (International) Ltd

Ewan Campbell
Campbell Properties

James Campbell
Reid Furniture Limited

Alasdair Campbell
AC Gold Services Ltd

Andy Campbell
Special Move

Lesley Campbell

Colin Carmichael
Pure Recruitment Solutions Ltd

Finlay Carmichael
C2 Software Ltd

David Carrick
Memex Technology Ltd

Peter Casebow
goodpractice.net

Alan Catto
The Technical Assistance Centre

Jus Chall
Forrestgate Developments

Nissim Chilton
SMI

Elie Chilton
The Company Creators

Laurie Clark
Anglo Scottish Concrete Holdings

Sir Arnold Clark
Arnold Clark Automobiles Ltd

Michael Clarke
The Buccleuch Estates Ltd

Lesley Collins
Edinburgh Investment Consultants

Paul Conway
Paul's Quality Butchers

Steve Cook
Linkfleet Limited

Jim Cooper

David Copeland
Bettingjobs.com

Norma Corlette
The Learning Game

Richard Corsie MBE
Corsie Group

Del Cotton
Hireaband Ltd

Graeme Cox
dns ltd

David Crosthwaite
DC Produce Direct Ltd

Terry Currie
Scottish Enterprise

Gary Daw
Daw Signs Limited

Gary Deans
KPMG

Sukhvir Dhillon
PriceYourMeal Ltd

Richard Dixon
Vets Now Ltd

Mike Donnelly
Gas Call Services Ltd

Tommy Dreelan
Dreelan Services Ltd

Maureen Dunlop
Commands

Bernard Dunn
MacDonald Reid Scott Group

Robin Dunseath

Garry Edwards
Midian Clinical Ltd

Lorna Edwards
Lawscript (Scotland) Ltd

Barrie Elder
Socomo Ltd

Richard Emanuel MBE
Interactive Telecom Solutions

Scott Fairgrieve
Change Homes Ltd

Sir Tom Farmer CBE
Maidencraig Ventures

David Farquhar
2in10 Limited

Richard Ferguson
Aitken & Niven

Graham Figes
Whitelaw Baikie Figes

Graham Filmer
Rocket Associates Ltd

Robert Findlay
Laurence McIntosh Ltd

Eric Flannigan
Flannigan Consulting

Bill Fleming
Science & Nature Ltd

Roy Flett
Legal Data Solutions Ltd

Tom Flockhart
Capital Solutions Ltd

Scott Forbes
Platinum Glass Design Ltd

Kylie Forrest
KL Events LLP

Angus Forsyth
City & Wharf Asset Management Ltd

Ron Forsyth
QaS Copak Ltd

Tricia Fox
Volpa Ltd

William Frame
Braemore Estates

Neil Fraser
QVision UK Ltd

Richard Freedman
ACS Clothing Ltd

June Friel
Electronic Media Publications Ltd

Eric Galbraith
Dundas & Wilson

Alasdair Gammack
SURE Ltd

Sir Bill Gammell
Cairn Energy Plc

Roy Gardner
Kennedy Construction Ltd

David Gardner
Run Deep Ltd

David Geddes
Obvious Solutions Ltd

Mark Gibson
Advanced Marketing Concepts

Jimmy Gilchrist
GP Plantscape Ltd

Charan Gill MBE
Harlequin Leisure Group Ltd

Steven Gillies
Isle of Skye Boatbuilders

Mario Gizzi
Windows Catering Co

Ann Gloag OBE
Stagecoach Group

Chris Gorman OBE

Nicholas Gould
Veecom Systems

Ian Grabiner
Arcadia Group

Iain Graham
Graham Technology plc

Robert Graham
Grahams Dairies Ltd

Cameron Grant
3x1

Andrew Grant
Nation1 Ltd

Hamish Grant
Axeon Ltd

Peter Grant
Grant Management Group

Colette Grant
Grant Management Group

Colin Gray
McGrigors.

Nelson Gray
Firth Ventures

Alistair Gray
First Genesis Ltd

Michael Gray OBE
Glenbrae Management Services Ltd

Stephen Gribben
International Training Network Ltd

Russel Griggs

Jonathan Guthrie
MGt plc

Alex Haddow
Objective Associates

John Hailstone
First People Solutions Group Ltd

Brian Halley
Slanj Scotland

Elaine Halley
Cherrybank Dental Spa

Stephen Halpin
Curious Group

Anne-Marie Hamill
E-Scape Recruitment Services Ltd

Ronald Hamilton
Provis Ltd

Roddy Hammond
Hammond Resources Ltd

John Harrison
Surfactant Technologies Ltd

Jim Harrold
WHM Engineering Ltd

Tessa Hartmann
The TFF Agency Ltd

Thomas Harwood
REL Group

William Haughey OBE
City Refrigeration Holdings Ltd

Kat Heathcote
Seamanship International

Ian Henderson
Rubric Ltd

Sue Holloway
Media Vision Ltd

Gavin Hollywood
Posterplus

Phil Holt
Run Deep Ltd

Bryan Hook
Hookson Limited

Lynne Hunter
Success Training (Scotland) Ltd

Sir Tom Hunter
West Coast Capital

Douglas Irvine
Irvine Group

Alastair Irvine
Irvine Group

Michael Jackson
WildDay.com

Roddy James
iicorr Ltd

Brian Johnston
Bank of Scotland

David Jones
Real Time Worlds

Jonathan Jones
Youth Media (UK)

Rachel Jones
Totseat Ltd

David Kaye
Clairmont Properties

Bruce Keith
3i Plc

Brian Kemp
United Freight Distribution

Ian Kennedy
Mediary Ltd

John Kennedy
Kenmore Property

Ian Kerr
ID Inquiries (Partnership)

Robert Kilgour
Dow Investments Ltd

Ian Kilpatrick
Prospects Group

Robert Kilpatrick
Prospects Group

Ronnie Klos
FFDR

Luigi Koechlin
Global Voices

Biju Krishnan
Scottish Dental Implant Centre

Vijay Kumar
Harveys Laundry

Aydin Kurt-Elli
Lumison

Susan Laing
Napier University

Campbell Laird
Three Brand Design Ltd

Ron Lander OBE
Scotlander plc

Margaret Lang
Intelligent Office UK Ltd

Greg Lavelle
Etellect Ltd

Iain Lawson
PPS (Scotland) Ltd

Gordon Lee
Parallel 56 Ltd

Craig Lemmon
2e-volve (UK) Ltd

James Leslie
Infinite Data Storage Ltd

Alasdair Locke
Abbot Group plc

Moir Lockhead OBE
First Group plc

David Lockwood

Alison Loudon
FWB Non-Executive

Charles Lovatt
LI Components Ltd

Stanley Lovatt
Bruce Group of Companies

Graeme Lowdon
ION Holdings Ltd

William Lowe
Saltire Taverns Ltd

Bruce Lyle

Colin Lynch
Blyth Construction Utilities Ltd

Donald Macdonald OBE
Macdonald Hotels

Morinne Macdonald
Macdonald Henderson

Jane Macdonald
Excel Vending Ltd

Grant MacIntyre
John MacIntyre & Son Ltd

Euan MacKenzie
3MRT Ltd

Douglas MacKenzie
hometech

Gordon MacKenzie
MacKenzie's (Cambuslang) Ltd

Ian MacLellan
MacLellan IT Ltd

Donald Macleod
DM Design Ltd

Iain MacRitchie
MCR Holdings

Sanjay Majhu
Harlequin Leisure Group Ltd

Andrew Malcolm
W H Malcolm Ltd

Andrew Martin
J G Martin Plant Hire Ltd

Paul Mason
iResponse Centres Ltd

Colin Mason
Hunter Centre for Entrepreneurship

Peter Matheson
Caledonian (Matheson) Airways Ltd

Steve Matthews
Alpha Plus (Scotland) Ltd

Andrew McAllister
RAD Software Ltd

Jim McAllister
JMC Wholesale Ltd

Kevin McCabe
Change Homes Ltd

Kai McCabe
Search Consultancy Ltd

Alan McCafferty
Balmore Holdings

John McCallum
McCallum Ceilings Ltd

Douglas McCarthy
McCarthy Travel Ltd

Jim McColl OBE
Clyde Blowers plc

Kimberley McCormick
Quartz Stone Carpets

Isla McCrone
Scottish Executive

David McCutcheon
Bullet Express

Wendy McDougall
9-20 Recruitment Ltd

Kevin McGechie
Print Squared

John McGlynn
Airlink Group

Michael McGonigle
Ollie Skatewear Ltd

Jim McGonigle
AJT Trading Ltd

Jennifer McGonigle
Ollie Skatewear Ltd

Mark McGowan
Bite (Scotland) Ltd

John McGuire
The Phoenix Car Co Ltd

David McInroy
Scottish Grass Machinery

Paul McKay
Arthur McKay & Co Ltd

Stephen McKechnie
Kelvin River Properties Ltd

Fiona McKelvie
Minotaur Magazines

Harvey McLean
Harvey McLean Ltd

Anne McLean
Sandalwood Shoes Ltd

Sharon McLean
The Home Staging Company

John McLeish
Equator (Scotland) Ltd

Sharon McLellan
Kissing With Confidence Ltd

Steven McLeod
Airth Castle Hotel & Spa Resort

Jim McMahon
West Coast Capital

Ian McMillan
Streamtec Ltd

Alison McRae
Blue Toucan

Patrick McTurk
XyRex Ltd

Jack McVitie
LEBC Group Ltd

Les Meikle
Wise Property Care Ltd

Callum Meikle
Fast Forward

John Meiklejohn
Strategem Ltd

Katherine Melton-Scott
Kathellan Fine Food and Gifts Ltd

Keith Miller CBE
The Miller Group

Stuart Miller
Young Enterprise Scotland

Amanda Miller
Project One FM

Stewart Milne
Stewart Milne Group Ltd

James Milne CBE
Balmoral Group Ltd

Ian Milton
Milton Hotel Group

Shona Mitchell
PeopleMatters (Europe) Ltd

Michelle Mone
MJM International Ltd

Andrew Montague
We Love Movies

John Morgan
Merle Limited

Iain Morgan
Active Corporate

Lynn Mortimer
Lynnet Leisure Ltd

David Moulsdale
Optical Express Ltd

Ian Murgitroyd
Murgitroyd & Company

Phil Murray
Petrotechnics Ltd

Iain Murray
Jenkins & Marr Facilities Management Ltd

Keith Neilson
Craneware Ltd

David Ness
Policy Services Ltd

Richard Nicol
Commsworld Holdings Ltd

Walter Nimmo

Glen Nimmo
Revera Asset Management Ltd

Oli Norman
DADA Events Ltd

Richard O'Connor
Ambergreen Internet Marketing

Hugh O'Donnell
DPM Water Technologies Ltd

Daniel O'Donnell
Connecti Ltd

Gillian O'Neil
Kginteractive

Marilyn Orcharton
Kite Holdings Ltd

Bill Park
Vibration Technology Ltd

Ronnie Park
SPH Property Search

Angela Paterson
Kite Ltd

Craig Paterson
Football Aid

Howard Perkins
Kyria Ltd

Andrew Pert

Anne Peters
Burnhouse Manor Hotel

Ray Phelan

Malcolm Phillips
Structural Composite Solutions Ltd

Jim Pickard
Accura Health Ltd

Sarah Playfair
Black Widow Racing

Keith Punler
Kapital Assets Ltd

Gordon Quinn
Campaign HQ Ltd

Jamie Rae
Redeem plc

Hans Ram
Platinum Sales & Marketing

Tarak Ramzan
Tarak Clothing Co Ltd

Maqbool Rasul
Global Video plc

Shaf Rasul
e-Net Computers Ltd

Asif Rasul
Outdoor World

Douglas Reid
RESCU Solutions Ltd

David Reid
1576 Advertising Ltd

Alan Revie
Axle Group Holdings Ltd

Eamonn Rice
Mform

Lucy Richards
StudioLR Ltd

Jim Richardson
SUMO Design

Isabel Ridley
Zebrano Ltd

Martin Ritchie
MR Ventures

Ian Ritchie
Coppertop Concepts Ltd

Stephen Ritchie
Enrich Group Ltd

Tamlin Roberts
Mercurytide Ltd

Hilary Roberts
HR Consultancy

Elliot Robertson
Manorlane Ltd

Roman Rock
Bedlam Event Management

John Roseman
Sematek Advanced Technology

Ann Rushforth
ScotNursing Ltd

Rita Rusk
Rita Rusk International

Andrew Russell
A&E Russell Ltd

Gordon Russell
All Signs Scotland

Sam Russell MBE
Simclar International Ltd

Mike Rutterford
Rutterford Ltd

John Scott
Scott Timber Ltd

Ilya Scott
Real PR Ltd

Louise Scott
Tidalfire Ltd

Louise Shafar
Louise Shafar Ltd

Khaled Shahbo
Enterprise Rent-a-Car UK Ltd

Ewan Shannon
Shannon Boardgames Ltd

Bill Sharpe
Stevenson Sharpe

Andrew Sharpe
Positive Care (Scotland) Ltd

Steven Shear
Studio Sixty

George Shepherd
Clark Thomson Shepherd Investors Ltd

David Sibbald
Sumerian Networks Ltd

Scott Simpson
Voltage Design Consultants Ltd

Charles Skene OBE
The Skene Group

Paul Slater
Slater Menswear

Duncan Smith
Fixeruppa Ltd

Maurice Smith
The Value Innovators

Michael Smith
ORB International KMS Ltd

Philip Smith
QPC Group

Alan Smith
Jobsat Ltd

Alison Smith
Activpayroll Ltd

Brian Souter
Stagecoach Group

Derek Souter
DJS Creative Marketing Ltd

John Speake
Company Growth Team

Gavin Speirs
Solutions Driven

Sara Speirs
Spectrum Service Solutions Ltd

Jim Sproat
CommunityPeople Ltd

Abigail Stevens
Think Global Recruitment Ltd

David Stevenson

Brian Stewart
Stewart Asset Management Group

Calum Stewart
SG Systems Ltd

Roddy Stewart
RS100

Chris Stewart
hometech

Sir Jackie Stewart OBE

Ron Stewart Snr
Andron Contract Services Ltd

John Stirling
Stirling Potatoes Ltd

Iain Stirling
Sunsol

Donald Storrie
Donald Storrie Group

Murray Strachan
The Petrofac Training Group

John Strachan
Maximillion Events Ltd

Mark Strudwick CBE
PSYBT

Gordon Stuart
Prospero

John Sturrock
Core Solutions Group Ltd

Anthony Sweeney
Consultiam

Tasos Symeonides
Axios Systems Ltd

James Taylor
P3 Music Ltd

Peter Taylor
The Town House Company

Charlie Taylor
Charlie Taylor Hair Design Ltd

Lisa Tennant
Greyhound Group

John Thompson
City Information Services Ltd

Andrew Thomson
Reservoir Management Ltd

Alasdair Thomson
Apax Partners

Ivor Tiefenbrun MBE
Linn Products Ltd

Chris Tiso
Graham Tiso Ltd

David Tobin
Dream Escape Ltd

James Turnbull
S x 3

Christiaan van der Kuyl
Tayforth Consulting Limited

Antonio Vezza
Suio UK

Rob Walker
Versko Ltd

Graham Wallace
Westica Communications Ltd

Liz Walsh
Wildfoods Ltd

Russell Wardrop
Kissing With Confidence Ltd

Clare Wareing
Nexus Oncology Ltd

John Waring
Pinpoint Ltd

Fergus Watson
Vets Now Ltd

John Watson
John Watson & Co Ltd

Alex Watts
Kingsford Estates Ltd

Graham Webster
G. H. Webster Ltd

Gerald Weisfeld
The Weisfeld Foundation

Anne Welby
Welby Healthcare

Michael Welch
Black Circles Ltd

Graeme White
Foxfire Marcoms Ltd

Gordon White
Design Matters

John Whyte
Interactive Telecom Solutions

Lesley Wiggins
Milne Management Ltd

Brian Williamson
The Learning Organisation

Alan Wiseman
Robert Wiseman Dairies plc

Leslie Wolfson

Kingsley Wood
Kilmacolm Property Centre Ltd

Sir Ian Wood CBE
John Wood Group plc

Caspian Woods
Editions Publishing

Colin Woodward
Contract Scotland Ltd

Frasia Wright
FWA (Scotland) Ltd

Jane Wylie-Roberts
Stafffinders

Eric Young
Eric Young & Co

Bill Young
Eastern Eagle Enterprises Ltd

Eddie Young
ACS (UK) Ltd

Steve Young
Aon Ltd